So Many Harp Seals

Katie Peters

GRL Consultant Diane Craig,
Certified Literacy Specialist

Lerner Publications ◆ Minneapolis

Note from a GRL Consultant
This Pull Ahead leveled book has been carefully designed for beginning readers. A team of guided reading literacy experts has reviewed and leveled the book to ensure readers pull ahead and experience success.

Lerner Publications
An imprint of Lerner Publishing Group, Inc.
241 First Avenue North
Minneapolis, MN 55401 USA

For reading levels and more information, look up this title at www.lernerbooks.com.

Main body text set in Memphis Pro 24/39
Typeface provided by Linotype.

Photo Acknowledgments
The images in this book are used with the permission of: © GlobalP/iStockphoto, p. 3; © HuntedDuck/iStockphoto, pp. 4–5; © AGAMI stock/iStockphoto, pp. 6–7; © slowmotiongli/iStockphoto, pp. 8–9, 16 (right); © neosummer/iStockphoto, pp. 10–11, 16 (center); © Michel VIARD/iStockphoto, pp. 12–13; © slowmotiongli/iStockphoto, pp. 14–15, 16 (left).

Front cover: © COULANGES/Shutterstock Images

Library of Congress Cataloging-in-Publication Data

Names: Peters, Katie, author.
Title: So many harp seals / Katie Peters.
Description: Minneapolis : Lerner Publications, [2025] | Series: Let's look at polar animals (pull ahead readers - nonfiction) | Includes index. | Audience: Ages 4–7 | Audience: Grades K–1 | Summary: "Harp seals can have many different traits. For example, they can be white or gray. Colorful photographs and engaging text help readers learn about seal features. Pairs with the fiction text, Harper and the Ice"—Provided by publisher.
Identifiers: LCCN 2023031596 (print) | LCCN 2023031597 (ebook) | ISBN 9798765626276 (library binding) | ISBN 9798765629338 (paperback) | ISBN 9798765634684 (epub)
Subjects: LCSH: Harp seal—Juvenile literature.
Classification: LCC QL737.P64 P425 2025 (print) | LCC QL737.P64 (ebook) | DDC 599.79/29—dc23/eng/20230717

LC record available at https://lccn.loc.gov/2023031596
LC ebook record available at https://lccn.loc.gov/2023031597

Manufactured in the United States of America
1 – CG – 7/15/24

Table of Contents

So Many Harp Seals

This seal is young.

This seal is old.

This seal is white.

This seal is gray.

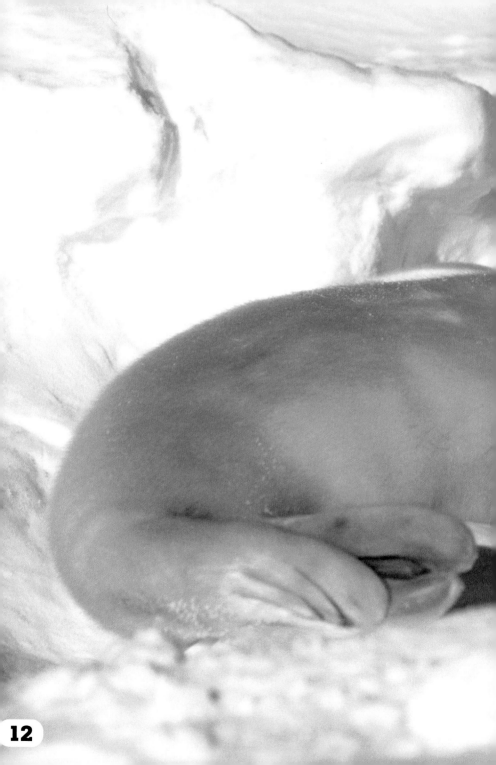

This seal is alone.

This seal is with its family.

Did You See It?

family

gray

white

Index